Alive and In Use

Poems in the Japanese Form of Haibun

Also by Charlotte Mandel

To Be the Daylight

Through a Garden Gate
(with photographs by Vincent Covello)

Life Work

Rock Vein Sky

Sight Lines

The Marriages of Jacob

Keeping Him Alive

The Life of Mary

Doll

A Disc of Clear Water

Saturday's Women
(editor, co-edited Maxine Silverman and Rachel Hadas)

Alive and In Use

Poems in the Japanese Form of Haibun

by

Charlotte Mandel

*To Maude,
with all good wishes,
Charlotte Mandel
September 2019*

Kelsay Books

Remembering Manny

and for our children

grandchildren

and great-grandchildren

Cover design by Shay Culligan
Cover photograph by Vincent Covello
Author photograph by Harold M. Shultz

ISBN: 978-1-949229-86-8

Library of Congress Control Number: 2019940072

Kelsay Books Inc.

kelsaybooks.com
502 S 1040 E, A119
American Fork, Utah 84003

Acknowledgments

With thanks to editors of the publications in which the following poems have appeared:

A Hundred Gourds: "Guilford Lake"
cattails: "A Fjord in Italy"; "Begonia"; "Garden Transactions";
    "Guardians"; "New York Moment"; "What Falls"
Contemporary Haibun Online: "Deciduous"; Mom and Pop
    Goat Farm"; "New Home on the Fourth of July";
    "Snow Maiden"
Failed Haiku: "Mantis Jaws"; "Memory of Henry";
    "Silky Pigtails, Photo Album"; "Traveling Circus"
Haibun Today: "Birdwatch at the Artists Colony"; "Domesticity";
    "Dreamers"; "My Neighborhood"; "Oak Grove";
    "Running Notes"; "Saratoga Springs Encounter";
    "The Last Farm Stand"
Modern Haiku: "September's First Monday"
    Awarded: Favorite Haibun, Issue 49.2
"Who Loves? (Somonka)"—epistolary lovers tanka exchange
    appears in my collection *Rock Vein Sky*
    (Midmarch Arts Press 2008); rpt. *Failed Haiku.*
    And gratitude to the late radiant Colette Inez who
    introduced me to the somonka form.

For generous advice and mentoring, I am tremendously grateful to Ray Rasmussen. Penny Harter introduced me to haibun. Others who inspire me and who keep these publications alive include Sonam Chhoki, Mike Montreuil, Mike Rehling, Roberta Beary, Bob Lucky, Terri French, Rich Youmans, Lorin Ford, Ruth Holzer, Melissa Allen, Glenn Coats, Jeffrey Woodward, Jim Kacian and Paul Miller.

Contents

Introduction

Scribbling freely in journals over the years, I wrote (still write) close observations of nature as well as happenings around me. Some of those writings evolve into prose poems, poems in free verse, formal received or nonce forms, and are especially useful now for haibun. The Japanese genre of haibun has attracted me for some time. The 17th-century poet Basho is regarded as seminal to the genre for his travel diary, *The Narrow Road to the Far North*. Sometimes called a hybrid because it combines the language of prose with that of verse, the haibun presents a concise prose section, which may be a natural scene, or a vignette of something which has happened. The prose then links to a haiku. The haiku may amplify tone or meaning, or shift direction to a surprise experience. A haiku must evoke associations which are not "told" but seem to be breathed into awareness. A haiku alone is brief, often lovely. A haibun offers language like a companion in thought—after prose images that present a three-dimensional world, the haiku takes the poem into a fourth dimension.

This collection's title expresses my gratitude to be able to discover by writing poems what I seek to know.

September's First Monday

Careful not to stumble on thick green sod, I stop and slowly bend
to pluck a dandelion still yellow among dozens with globes of
blow-away seeds. Holding the rubbery thread of stem between
thumb and forefinger, I inhale scents of grass and earth cleansed
by last night's rain. Sun-warmed downy petals stroke my cheek.
The flower's crown wobbles.

fontanel pulse
in the cup of my hand
once

A Fjord in Italy: Lake Como

Mountains like a series of fans form a backdrop to the long
span of gray-blue undulating water. A snow-covered peak
picks up the sun, brilliant fire on white. Fog remnants travel
lazily, like clouds disconnected from earth or lake surface.

All are shades of blue—mountains, mist, water—deepest blue
seen through a cutwork of openings left by evaporating clouds.

Rose afterglow tints the clouds, darkening their reflections
on the lake. The peaks sparkle, lustrous.

dawn glow   granite   transforms to opal

Mountain's Gift

On our visit to Acadia National Park in Maine, we drive as far as allowed to the high granite peak of Cadillac Mountain, then hike a mile to the summit. Above the tree/foliage line, we walk on bare speckled gray rock. Sitting side by side on a convenient outcropping, we gaze at the panoramic view. In a moment, my husband reaches out. A small plant seems to sprout directly out of granite. He plucks the sprig, hands it to me like a love bouquet, and we nibble the half-dozen small wild blueberries.

hidden wiry root
sweetness again

Birdwatch at the Artists' Colony (Yaddo)

Tonight, dinner table talk buzzes about the great blue heron sighted in one of four ponds enclosed by tall woods and thorny shrubs. Raised in Brooklyn, New York, I'd never seen the bird wild or even in a zoo.

"Where? Where did you spot it—which lake?" I ask successful finders.

"The one just past the composer's cottage" or "as you come around the waterfall" or "the one where the child drowned last century."

I can't interpret the directions, but on my daily walks on the hard dirt road through the woods, I scan each small body of water hoping for sight of the famous creature, not sure I'd recognize a great blue heron if I did see one.

After three weeks, on the morning of my return home, I walk my last round, taking deep breaths of the pine-fresh air, my quest nearly forgotten. At the fourth pond, I glance right—and there stands the great bird, wading in shallow water thickly scummed with yellow-green algae. A bird almost my own height, he seems a throwback from the dinosaur era. Feathers grey as sky about to storm, beak yellowish, long, thick, with a dagger point.

The heron lifts stick-thin legs, sets them down again, reaches a serpent-like neck and snaps up a sunfish. His sharp beak pulps the prize enough to be swallowed at one gulp. His eyes, black beads encircled in gold and black, just above each side of the beak, scan surrounding woods.

eye to eye
motionless
with the heron

Saratoga Springs Encounter

Green algae clog the lake nourished by waste toxins from
the racetrack. I walk past on the edge of the highway toward
the track entrance. Just after sunrise, I've come out to see the
horses exercised. On the public road lodges an old tortoise with
filthy toenails, mud-colored fungus on odoriferous shell,
thick body and toothless sharp beak.

"Are you dead?" I shout, and stamp my foot to get a rise out of it.
The left front foot stirs. "Get out of the road!" Not the slightest
movement. "I don't want you to be hit by a car!" The front knee
bends. I stamp in staccato thumping. "Move!" Two more knees
bend, then a fourth and the creature drags an inch forward.
I stamp, it drags itself forward, leaving a wet greenish trail on
the pavement until flopped on the grass border. The sun is high.

slow trek
from toxic lake
hot asphalt

Guilford Lake

A young boy named Ken sat upon the stone wall at lake's edge
today, fishing for bass, catching only sunnies and throwing them
 back. One came up deeply hooked and when the boy tugged,
worse happened—it held. I saw that he had no sense of working
the hook out gently—as I might work an earring through my ear
lobe—and much blood came upon the boy's hand, his left hand.
Loosening the fish at last, he threw it back. Worried, though:
"He's not dead, he didn't come up—if he dies, he'll float."

"He'll heal," I said, almost sure of this. Telling myself you
 can't pity every damn thing that somebody hurts in this world.

But I didn't like to see the boy left with a bloody hand.
"Do you want me to get you some water to wash that or do you
 want to put it in the lake?" I gave him a leading question
of choices.

swirl of red
on green current
mouths wide open

Domesticity

September's blue sky feels freshly laundered, a few white
clouds hung up to dry in sun after yesterday's rain. Foliage
of trees on the opposing bank of the pond doubled by water's
mirror. Heavy-footed geese curve long necks to tear grass
from the sloping bank, having led their adolescent young out of
summer's nesting woods. Flapping their wings, rustling tail
feathers, they waddle down to the mossy water, rows of goslings
following, one by one, with scarcely a splash.

my new jacket and the grass
green ripples

New York Moment

Over my open paperback *Duino Elegies* purchased in of all places
Port Authority Bus Terminal, a card is thrust. I meet the dancing
look of a lithe young man, mirth in the recesses of his eyes
scarcely shadowed by a large-brimmed hat, his jacket glove-fitted
to the V of his waist. Beneath his card floats a phrase of Rilke's
prose:
"...one's left with a mere intimation of the kind of speech that
may be possible There, where silence reigns..."

HELLO! I AM A DEAF PERSON say the words beside a dove
with wings of an eagle, olive branch in the hook of its beak, flying
over wind-flapping stars and stripes. I AM SELLING THIS and
now sans serif shifts to italic with flowing capitals matching
the flag's brash insouciance: *Pay Any Price You Like.*

It was a moment brought still—I and the mute cardbearer
motionless in that spot.

groans of the city's
millions of engines
jingle of my fifty cents

Apartment Balcony, New York City

From my second-floor balcony I watch the morning's walkers
on their way to work or school. My view of the building across
the street is prefaced by crowns of three trees in full leaf. Two
maples spread branches that form a network canopy of shade.
The tall gingko between is one of the oldest species on earth.
Its leaves cluster close to a narrow white spine.

man in wide-brimmed hat
twin granddaughters
hand in hand

The heartbeat of a city does not pulse but rolls like perpetual
thunder—a blend of humming airconditioners, intermittent
barking of dogs, squealing brakes, wheel rush of a taxicab.

Indoors, I sink onto down-filled couch cushions. Shut windows
banish the city. On the wall, an ancient Japanese print depicts
two women in kimonos crossing a wooden bridge over tranquil
water.

framed under window glass
cityscape

Silky Pigtails: Photo Album

My little girls and I wear flower print sundresses—mother and daughter dresses are a popular fashion—especially for mothers still in their twenties. The girls, ages seven and three, intent over a game on sandy ground. The snapshot shows their backs and delicate arms pushing an oval stone with twigs.

I've parted their hair down the back into two sections, each divided by my fingers into three strands, weaving center strand down, right one over, then left, fastened at the ends with plastic daisy barrettes. The older girl's red-gold hair heavier texture, the younger's shining brown with tint of gold highlights in the sun, fine as embroidery threads.

My hands do not weave their future.

peach tree buds
tight silk
no way to hasten fragrance

Memory of Henry

As the living room in my daughter's apartment cools to the
humming air conditioner, Henry enters on feathery paws padding
noiselessly over polished wood flooring. His forehead, an inverted
triangle of black above white fur, traces a line to the corners of
his eyelids, giving him exotic beauty. He fills a chair with pillowy
black and white grace, jewel eyes fixed upon my face, unblinking.
I'm soothed by this cat's desire for my companionship.

on the kitchen floor
a blue plastic bowl
empty

Solstice Midnight

Morning's radio announces this will be the first full moon to coincide with summer solstice since 1967. At dusk, a pale disc appears half-hidden by cloud as though rising above a range of hills. A jet plane taking altitude writes twin white tracks on the darkening sky. As blue shadows blend into black, the full moon bursts forth, radiating halo that glows over fading jet stream and breeze-born shreds of cloud.

blare of a white trumpet
moonflower

Firelight At Twilight

I've kindled the wood provided for the country inn bedroom's
stone fireplace. Rose-yellow flames slide shadows along
the walls. Half undressed, I lie on an embroidered pillow on
the four-poster bed, snuggled under a patchwork quilt.
Fresh-picked red apples fill a blue bowl on the bedside table.
Winey aroma blends with the odor of flame-spitting pine logs.

The door opens to my beloved's return, his face aglow with
delighted surprise.

dusk presses on drawn blinds
uplifted arms

Dreamers

In the dream, my husband says he wants to leave me and
nothing I say—to charm or to threaten—can change his mind.
He's adamant, unsmiling, even contemptuous. We're driving
home and I shout, "Stop the car—let me out!" He shrugs
and applies the brake. The landscape is a flat brown desert
stretched to a clouded horizon.

I wake up, afraid there's some truth in the dream and hear him
saying unintelligible words in his sleep. Is he dreaming about
leaving me? I shake him awake—" what are you dreaming?"
"Hm? Nothing."

"Yes, you were talking in your sleep. I dreamt you were
leaving me. Please don't ever leave me!"

"I won't, but I have to right now, to go to the bathroom."

border checkpoint
no ASL
dictionary

Workdays at Millay Colony

In the field of browning grass and reddening weeds, stands
a white pine tree the height of my breastbone. I stroke a branch.
The summer grown needles feel soft as the fur of the orange
cat who visits my barn studio.

licks of rough tongue
Chopin on radio

The view spreads before me like outstretched arms ready
to embrace, the sky cloudless blue. Two pale yellow butterflies
dance together over green meadow—keeping distance, spinning
apart and then into a startled do-si-do. Country dance all about
me—flamenco hands of red maple leaves, sway of feather spruce
and long-needled white pine. Breeze conducted chorus of
goldenrod, wild carrot, an expanse of tall grasses about to be cut,
dried and bound into bales of hay.

ready for harvest
scribbled pages

My Neighborhood

Kerchiefs tied around their heads, two small old women
with long-handled brooms are bending over their asphalt
driveway. One terrified of the other, her voice scarcely above
a whisper, the other battling for her delusions, shouting
complaint about their neighbor next door.

"He throws these things over onto me!" She's talking about
the neighbor's maple tree dangling yellow flower-fringes which
shower and scatter onto the ground in early spring. No way to
direct the wind, but she blames him for littering her land, and rants
to any passerby as back and forth she sweeps.

A young man in a reversed-bill baseball cap comes out of the
house next door. He goes straight to the red car parked at the curb,
a rocket-nosed low-end sports model, and zooms off.

windblown seeds
chase a thrumming
hot engine

The Park At Vernal Equinox

School holiday week. Children emerge like petals on the weeping cherry. I choose a bench facing the lake. White swan boats nest beside the boathouse. The grassy lawn has invited an amorous couple, close together on a plaid blanket. He strokes her hair, she hums.

Canada geese honk
mating season

A parade passes before me on the paved path that circles the lake —young mother pushing a twin stroller, then a sextet of middle school girls in jeans and multicolored scarves, playfully cuffing one another as they skip and giggle. Varieties of dogs—a yipping bundle of white fringes, one whose Great Dane size head menaces on a boxer body, a large shaggy gray poodle in need of a barber.

drawn upward in sun
my face a vortex

Begonia

Fallen from the plant on the dining table, the tiny flower spreads two petals, pale pink, on either side of the yellow-brown center. A bit of stem holds on. I lift the threadlike stem between thumb and forefinger, careful not to crush the already wrinkling soft-skinned miniature blossom. Is it still alive though no longer able to feed from the taproot?

heartbeats
silent
on the monitor screen

Turned over, the petal-wings seem less shriveled, more rounded, edged as with a rolled hem. Odor of a cotton ball, taste of bitter weeds. My gentle fingers cause a tear.

her face being scrubbed
the child winces
but does not cry

On the palm of my hand, the moth-like petals turn browner by each tick of the digital clock blinking its two-dotted eye. I place it back in the ceramic pot, onto damp earth shaded by a leafed stem bearing buds about to open.

my husband's ashes
buried beside
a tall pine tree

Chosen Site

Near to the garden's sound of waterfall, we bury his ashes.
Our sons and grandsons together dig a square at root margin
of the newly transplanted monumental pine. The labeled box
is set within the opening and covered with earth. An engraved
stone plaque marks the place not to be trodden on:
To where has he passed?
A tall pine
Evergreen on the highest peak

At this site, he would take his calmest deepest breaths.
Voices murmur love and goodbye. I stay.

a tall pine tree's shadow
listening

Guardians

A day to walk in pleasant breeze. White clouds drifting in the blue sky alternately cover and allow the sun through. I walk across grass to the cedar bench overlooking the pond. The woods beyond form a haze of early green leaves. Two fountain sprays create soothing waterfall sounds.

sunfish leaps
to catch a damselfly
brief whirlpool

A pair of Canada geese rest on the water, accepting my seated presence. One is larger than the other, I judge them husband and wife. I've been told these birds mate for life.

five years gone. . .
he still smiles
in the framed photo

The geese glide to the water's edge and leap onto the grass bank. One grazes, pulling green blades one at a time. The larger bird climbs up the slope, stretches its long neck and stands rigid, only eyes moving, on guard. A few minutes later, this one comes down to graze and the other climbs up to post watch. As I leave, they continue to take turns.

Deciduous

The maple stands in orange-tinted confusion, leaves in strong
wind hitting against one another, but clinging to twig and branch.
Leaf colors—reds, yellows, mauves—are lasting longer because
of unusual summer warmth. In its thirty years since planting, the
tree followed a schedule that matched my calendar time, leaves
beginning to turn celebratory color in late September, floating to
earth on October winds, bare by mid-November's chill. The
outermost leaves spread out like hands of a person asking
"what am I to do now?"

red leaves following ski tracks

Rocking Chair Angel

In this wing of the retirement home, a lounge room next to the
elevator is furnished like a sun porch with wicker chairs and couch.
Sunlight pours through the windows. Flowered print chintz
cushions enhance my sense of being in a garden. A pillowed
 rocker holds me in its arms, welcome warmth on back of my head.
A woman steers her walker to the elevator adjacent. "Your hair,"
she says, "is a halo in the sun." The elevator door slides open, she
passes through, it slides shut.

dust in a ray of sun
fireflies

Who Loves? (Somonka)

Somonka: lovers epistolary tanka exchange

Your letters deceive—
every syllable reveals
*   you won't return.*
Seated at your polished desk,
whoever enters must bow.

Such a fantasy!
no one bows down to me here.
        How to convince you?
Must I lap milk from the bowl
of your kindness each day?

I long for brushed lines
that subtly caress the page,
*   i's dotted with moonlight.*
Today I saw white herons
doubled in calm reflections.

This city offers
neither bird nor sunny lake.
        I crouch in a room
without windows, overhear
pigeons cooing on gargoyles.

And what do they say?
Do you imagine lovespeak
*   roosting two by two?*
Squirrels are building a nest
in the crown of our maple.

The computer hums
like a strict instructor
        ordering fingers
to play musical keyboard,
a letter always missing.

Remember the school
where we met as first graders?
Voices of children
shrill as whistling teakettles,
rumps slip-sliding down the chute!

The seesaw asked for
two bodies alike in weight—
we weren't a match
and forgot each other's names.
Now yours is my mind's default.

Computer jargon
as metaphor? Explain, please.
Song of the forties?
"I see your face before me...."
on billboards, night and day dreams?

Echoing voices
conspiratorial hiss
a hum of whispers
breaths held on audiofile
a flashing funhouse mirror.

A mother loon swims
with hatchling on her shoulder—
the bit of brown fluff
serene, blue lake accepted
as floor, blue sky as ceiling.

Parental fealty
Ah—infant's Edenic trust
casements wide open
cherubic zephyrs at play
doors innocent of padlocks.

Xylophone bell-notes
Lips blowing rosy bubbles
*   Conch shells inner satin*
Caribbean turquoise tides
Why not conjure sweet-salt dreams?

Now my telephone
interrupts like a jailer
        time to do this/that/
clang! crash!   burr in the eardrum!
lyrical thoughts? Forget it!

Come back with me, then—
Let machines talk to machines.
*   When my body speaks*
your phantom blood courses through—
heat and pulse and loss of self

yes, and gain! Kisses
articulate, words arouse
        something within me
wild for the *You* questioning/
answering within my veins.

Garden Transactions

Slow to bloom through the long hot summer, overnight the butterfly bush radiates cone-shaped panicles of white petals. Each tiny flower has a nectar-filled tube just right for butterflies and hummingbirds.

First to arrive is a ruby-throated hummingbird, vibrating its iridescent gauze-like wings as it hovers to sip. Two minutes later, a dozen purple swallowtail butterflies seek out the bush, covering white petals with translucent fluttering, crowding out the bird. When the hummingbird flits to a nearby flower, three of the butterflies follow and drive it away. The bird tries a different flower and again the butterfly team pursues. The hummingbird wings itself backward, lifts into air and swoops to a small plant with a reddish tubular flower that resembles a shrimp. Thirsty tongues unwind.

after nectar   in the flower's heart   gold dust

Garden Coexistence

My daughter in a blue smock has been pruning, weeding, gathering discarded twigs and branches. With her blonde shoulder length swish-about hair, she's a gold and blue animate creature among greens of grass and leaves, yellows and whites of hibiscus and star hydrangea. She lifts her head, frowning as the landscaper's pickup truck rattles on the gravel driveway. Heavy grasscutting machinery assaults the garden with loud motor vibration. A yellow-rumped warbler on the patio begins to hop about in lopsided circles, uttering a chirp every half minute.

chek   chek   chek
lawnmower crew in earmuffs

Midsummer Guests

After several rainy seasons, my daughter and son-in-law have
trimmed thick overgrowth to create a garden of "golden shade"—
an expanse of plantings that do well in shade. At the foot of a tall
umbrella pine, a border of pale lavender hosta. At the far end,
a line of hydrangea unfurl greenish-white globes, not yet ripened
into blue. Fluttering wings of a large white butterfly and a black-
capped chickadee seek out the same climbing vine, a white-pink
clematis. Pachysandra in healthy full summer growth bedeck
the edge of the porch where I sway on a blue-cushioned glider,
glass of lemonade in hand.

in a dry season   deep roots quench thirsts

Mantis Jaws

Wings folded against the long slim oval of its midsection,
the green mantis climbing the outside of the porch screen
ignores my outstretched hand. It climbs at right angles, across,
then straight upwards, thread-like legs using the screen's metal
squares as a ladder, head turning from side to side searching
for prey.

Hanging upside down, extended forelegs capture a yellow jacket.
At tip of the mantis's rod-like upper thorax, its triangular head
moves up and down, jaws at work. Little by little, the paralyzed
wasp is drawn backwards into the mantis's mouth, the black
bead of its head last to be seen.

wasp trachea
pulped
my clenched teeth

Mom & Pop Goat Farm, NY State

On this hand-operated farm of fifty goats, the family work round the clock. Breeding, raising, medicating, twice-daily milking, sanitizing cheesemaking utensils.

At entrance stands a gallon size hourglass-shaped jar. The jar's tight cover is perforated—holes towards which flies are lured by odors of rot and decay, stinks adored by manure feeders who swarm into the goats' corral. A wriggling black mass fills more than half the jar—close-packed bodies, those at the bottom smothered by the steadily increasing weight of fellow-creatures.

lunch
whole grain bread
fresh white cheese

Traveling Circus, New Jersey, 1994

On this chilly May morning, the Cole Bros-Clyde Beatty Circus
attracts few onlookers to its tent-raising. The big old elephant
named Pete is working, his strength harnessed to raise the heavy
canvas roof and walls attached to a center and six outer poles.
Pete is led past us. The edges of his ears look damaged—bleached,
mottled, ragged. Enormous, he seems a mountain given grace
of mobility.

deepset eyes
rimmed by wrinkles
shackled ankles

A group of children, six to nine years old, arrive walking in a file,
two by two, each holding to a rope passed down the center, front
end held by a woman, back end by a man. The children have
hearing, vision, or neurological disabilities. None are wearing
sweaters.

The adults concentrate on the action of shepherding to avoid
animal dung, jackhammer trucks, electrical cables being laid.

caged tiger
eyes on children
holding the rope

New Home on the Fourth of July

From my balcony, I watch fireworks shooting up from the high
 school football field a half-mile away. The wooden floor under
my feet shudders. I shiver to a sharp whistling whine each time
a pole of light shoots upward to explode into showers of crackling
colored lights—red, green, white globes and banners of fire. But
at the first sudden burst of sound, mockingbirds, finches and doves
driven from sleep in their summer nests fly at top speed past my
view. Jets of light strafe the sky, my ear drums vibrate to boom
after boom.

smoke trails vaporize
nestlings' beaks
strained open

Night Walk, Retirement Home

Deserted corridor. Every door guards a sleeper. Ceiling lights dimmed. Only I and the security watchman, metal ring of eighty keys on his belt, pass these doors tonight. Why am I not, like others, in night clothes under a quilt?

I want to breathe cool air, gaze at the three-quarter moon stroked by wisps of cloud, but fear nocturnal animals of any species, even my own. Around my neck a pendant reassures—thumb press and "security" (Paul tonight) will rush to me.

I carry a notebook and pen in a wool tote bag. The creaking elevator takes me down to the lobby atrium. Lights are off in the dining room and cafe, the front desk computer sleeps.

rasp of a pen
on blue ruled lines
lips reading

Running Notes

Today marks the annual New York City marathon, with runners
numbering fifty-one thousand, nine hundred ninety-five. The
radio station "Classical New York, WQXR" is playing a parallel
"marathon" of all nine Beethoven symphonies. With the television
set on mute, I'm watching the runners while listening to the radio
music. The fifth comes on, opening chords matching Morse code's
V for Victory.

breaking yellow tape
the crowd's
open mouths

Suburban Habitat

This morning before breakfast, taking my exercise walk on the
sidewalk bordering the traffic avenue, I was stopped in mid-step.
A killed fawn lay in my path, upper body on grass, small hooves
on pavement. The symmetrical print pattern of its sides, intended
for protective coloration in the woods, did not assist when
following its mother doe across a four-lane thoroughfare.

It lay in profile, features small and delicate, open eye a sharply
defined oval, thin cheek tapered to closed mouth scarlet as though
dipped into a burning stream, holding moment of shock.

wail of police siren
the doe's swollen nipples

Snow Maiden

In winter, our kitchen window served as an extra icebox. The wide wooden sill supported a galvanized tin lidded box perfect for storing bottles of milk, cottage cheese and sour cream. Sweet cream to pour over my chocolate pudding was available as "top milk"—cream that separated and rose to the top unless the bottle were energetically shaken. With hard work, the cream could be beaten into near butter.

The window served also as beauty aid. At first snow, my mother opened the window, filled her palm with the white cold fluff, and washed it over my face. This, she said, was for the complexion, to guarantee rosy cheeks. It must have been effective—my school friends accused me of wearing rouge before we were allowed to use makeup.

snowflakes
white lace
on a tenement sill

Parking Lot Antarctica

Zero degrees today, wind chill minus 12. Keeping the car battery alive when temperature plummets requires revving up the engine and driving at least twenty minutes. To keep myself alive I would beg to stay indoors, but follow the auto mechanic's warning, bundle into my long coat lined with faux fur, slide behind the wheel, and insert the ignition key.

life rattle
humming
neighborhood tour

Snow Battle of the Sexes

I'm fourteen, walking the eight blocks from my high school
between banks of freshly cleared powder snow. In my royal
blue hooded coat, I hug my books against my chest in the way
of most girls. Boys usually swing their books from a leather
strap. A dozen boys, about ten or eleven years old, are pitching
snowballs in teams over the street, sheltering behind packed
fortresses of snow. My path will take me in the line of fire.
"Watch out for the lady!" one calls out, and at once the boys stop
the fight and wait for me to pass.

As I come nearer, their perspective changes: "That's not a lady,
that's a girl!" and snowballs start to fly at machine gun speed.
Head down, I run past.

numb frostbitten nose
sweaty armpits

Oak Grove

I've taken my grandsons, five and seven years old, to visit
great-grandpa at his senior residence. He and I sit on lawn chairs
watching them play about the yard, an area of grass and trees
with thick gnarled trunks. Acorns cover the ground like round
berries on a tart.

"You can't catch me, Nana!" True, I cannot catch either of them
unless they wish me to. Acorns covering the surface of the slope
sound with a crunch underfoot. A squirrel on a gray branch
watches, motionless. A breeze ruffles the bush of its tail.

A slight chill rides on the breeze. I give my father a hand as he
pulls himself up from the deep wooden chair.

shadows lengthen. . .
his bony shoulder
under my hug

Talking to Anyone/No One

My father who lives in a small old age home has been brought
to the hospital with a stroke and I've rushed to be with him. His
often confused friend Helen, who depends upon him to keep her
oriented, calls my number over and over again, answered each
time by the recorded message on the answerphone. I come home to
her several voice messages on the tape:

—*I wanna know what Louie is doing. I wanna talk to Louie's
      daughter.*
—*Where is Louie? I can't wait so long I don't get no answer.*
—*I just wanna know how Louie is doing. He is my good friend
      and I don't know how he is doing now. Please let me
      know how he is.*
—*Hello. I'm Helen, Louie's neighbor. I would like to know how
      he is doing we were very close friends before. And nobody
      lets me know how he is doing. Please tell me.*
—*Hello hello. I can't get any answer from anyone how he is
      doing. Please tell 783..........*
      [Confused mixup of numbers].
—*Louie's daughter please answer me. I'm waiting right
      here by the phone. Please answer me. Thank you.*
—*What is this already?* [She's getting angry at the taped
      meaningless message.]
—*Are you Louie's doctor?*
—*Hello hello hello*
CLICK
      [The tape is used up.]

keys moving in tune
on a player piano
ghost hands

The Last Farm Stand

Baskets of apples line up on the low porch of a white frame house, prices crayoned on cardboard squares tacked to wooden sticks. The porch creaks with my step, and out comes the tender of this orchard—tall, lean, whitehaired. Word-thrifty. The macouns attract me with their sharp-sweet fragrance, their red color striped with green at the stem. The man upturns the basket's apples into a brown paper bag. The front door opens again. A gaunt woman emerges in faded print cotton dress and loose cardigan, white hair in a braided bun. The man stands, arms hanging down. When I open my purse, the woman puts out an arthritic knuckled hand, palm up. I hand her four dollar bills that she quickly folds into a pocket of her sweater. From the other pocket, she fingers two quarters for my change and drops them into the cup of my palm.

Halfway to my car parked on the dirt road, I pass a pile of cut up logs next to a tree stump, its diameter the length of my arm. An aroma of fresh cut wood.

sawdust caught in metal teeth
a century of tree rings

What Falls

This maple leaf, the color of pinot noir, lies like a five-pointed
star on green lawn. Underside, the leaf raises a central vein. Four
smaller veins branch out like capillaries at evenly spaced intervals.
Through the tree's inner pipeline, the leaf in summer drinks water
traveling from the roots and, in turn, feeds hormones for growth.
Each vein plays a part in nurture of the tree.

my daughter and I
bend to the crib
first grandchild

The fallen leaf grows drier, more brittle. On my palm, it begins
to curl.

my father's hand
holding mine
last visit

About the Author

Charlotte Mandel has published ten books of poetry, the most recent, *To Be the Daylight* from Kelsay Books. Previous titles include *Through a Garden Gate,* poems in response to photographs of the garden created and photographed by Vincent Covello, *Sight Lines, Rock Vein Sky, Life Work,* and two poem-novellas of feminist biblical revision—*The Life of Mary* and *The Marriages of Jacob.* Her awards include the 2012 New Jersey Poets Prize, two fellowships in poetry from New Jersey State Council on the Arts, residence fellowships at Yaddo, Millay Colony, Virginia Center for Creative Arts, and Villa Montalvo. She edited the Eileen W. Barnes Award Anthology, *Saturday's Women.* Her critical essays include a series on the role of cinema in the life and work of H.D. (Hilda Doolittle). She recently retired from teaching poetry writing at Barnard College Center for Research on Women.

Visit her at charlottemandel.com.